A LITTLE GESTE

AND OTHER POEMS

A Little Geste

AND OTHER POEMS

Daniel G. Hoffman

New York · OXFORD UNIVERSITY PRESS · *1960*

Library of Congress Catalogue Card Number 60–13208
Printed in the United States of America

Again,
for E. McF. H.

ACKNOWLEDGMENT is made to the editors of the following publications in which certain of the poems in this book first appeared: *Beloit Poetry Journal; Carleton Miscellany; discovery; Furioso; Hudson Review; Ladies' Home Journal; New Republic; New World Writing; Paris Review; Partisan Review; Saturday Review; Transatlantic Review;* and particularly, *Sewanee Review,* edited by Monroe K. Spears.

Contents

POEMS AND BLESSINGS

In the Beginning	3
Heraldry	5
The Everlasting	6
In a Cold Climate	7
Islands	9
Exploration	12
The Hermit of Cape Rosier	14
The Beech Tree	17
Cowhead	19
In Cytherea	21
Safari	23
In the Days of Rin-Tin-Tin	25
Pot aux Foux	26
A Black-Letter Broadside	27
The Augury	28
Flushing Meadows, 1939	30
Starlight	32
Awoke into a Dream of Singing	33
A Rainride	34
Sources	35
Scholiast / Iconoclast	36
A Triumph	37
The Blessings	38

TALIESIN

I	Wry Bread	45
II	Taliesin Sings	46
III	Divinations of Taliesin	46
IV	Taliesin's Revelations	52

A LITTLE GESTE

I	Near Nottingham	63
II	Chant	64
III	Aubade	65
IV	The Lay of Marian	67
	Much	67
	Will Scarlet	69
	Tuck	72
V	The Coming of Robin Hood	75
VI	Robin Hood and the Prioress	80
VII	Tuck, in the Stocks	82
VIII	A Carol of the Birds	85

POEMS AND BLESSINGS

'I, at this time,
Saw blessings spread around me like a sea.'

—WORDSWORTH, *The Prelude*

In the Beginning

On the jetty, our fingers shading
incandescent sky and sea,

my daughter stands with me.
'Boat! Boat!' she cries, her voice

in the current of speech cascading
with recognition's joys.

'Boat!' she cries; in spindrift
bobbling sails diminish,

but Kate's a joyous spendthrift
of her language's resources.

Her ecstasy's contagion
touches the whirling gulls

and turns their gibbering calls
to 'Boat! Boat!' Her passion

to name the nameless pulls her
from the syllabic sea

of incommunicate loneliness,
from the isles of infancy.

She points beyond the jetty
where the uncontested sun

wimples the wakeless water
and cries, 'Boat!' though there is none.

But that makes no difference to Katy,
atingle with vision and word;

and why do I doubt that the harbor,
in the inner design of truth,

is speckled with tops'ls and spinnakers,
creased with the hulls of sloops?

Kate's word names the vision
that's hers; I try to share.

That verbal imagination
I've envied, and long wished for:

the world without description
is vast and wild as death;

the word the tongue has spoken
creates the world and truth.

Child, magician, poet
by incantation rule;

their frenzy's spell unbroken
defines the topgallant soul.

4

Heraldry

Beneath the bull
Barns bulge fodder-full.
Iron Indian or Devil
Over oaths, rum and ale
Straddles smoked gable.
Stallion on stable,
Barque spun by stays'l
Tops shipcaptain's hall.
At South Penobscot, a whale
Crowns a cupola, tail
Churning skyswell
Though the harpooneers dwell
Under stone on the hill.
On Little Deer Isle,
Clapboard and humble
Yet crowned with a cockerel
And proud stands the chapel;
Its barnyard archangel
In golden apparel
Turns sunfierce fantail
As the wind veers at will.
Inshore rears the steeple
Spearing a mackerel
Silhouette, sacerdotal
In act, and used well—
Thus thrice-beautiful.

The Everlasting

We went out on a meadow in a mote of the sun
waist-high in the yarrow
gathering pearly everlasting.

On the hilltop we gathered the luminous stems,
luminous flowers
cloudwhite as though holding the sun's light within.

We brought a full basket down the cow's-foot-plashed trail
where eared with a targe
a green frog disappeared in a hoof-deep pool.

That summer sped by as the corntassels climbed;
the patient dray, shod
where the smith's sparks gonged in the deep shed's shade;

the splash and shudder as the iced stream swirled
diving under the dam
bright pebbles and foam; the night-crazed loon

forcing his agony on the crisp dark. . .
The white everlasting
dried in the vase.   By Christmas it stood

lightless and stark, prickly in pallor,
the husk of brightness.
The splendid energy of summer

glows in the everlasting still
in pearls of light
on yarrowy fields that scrape the sun.

6

In a Cold Climate

Pastures where the grass round granite grows
and not immoderate greenness gives homage
to the long fight with clutched root and snowcap

with the sun near and spoondrift in the wind, and cows
licking sunbaked snowsalt crusts on stones,
hooves akimbo under the bright etched map

of tropical isles in the goldribbed sky all summer
bespeak, in the noonheat, the rigor of cold climates,
as fishspine shoals, sunbleached when the tide's out, show

the integrity of bone.   Who would encumber
these huckleberryfields' sparse opulence with tropics'
richesse?   Wise clouds withhold vermilion snow.

The seals who surface at the cove's mouth
almost serve to humanize the seascape;
or does the unfootprinted pebbly shore

remind the poised osprey and the dun calf
that soft-eyed swimmers wreathed in ripplerobes
may be Poseidon's myrmidons, that here

is present but one representative
alien by birthright's will to those who ply
by fin, pinion, hoof, the unremitting

elements in whose brief grace they live,
whose almost-mastered impulse is to try
bending to the will's way the living, the unliving?

I invoke the instinctual wisdom of the hawk's wing,
the dumb cow's long-tongued patience, the seals'
handwebbed finesse in motion indivisible

from the cold seas', joyous in their submitting
to the tide's seasons and turn, leaving my heels'
prints on the shore, visible or invisible.

Islands

Springtide noon's low-watermark:
the glazed heat's haze
makes space dissolve; the near, the far

islands are indistinguishable;
buoytowers stand stark upright; spars
hang in the air.   Now all is still.

Seeming no nearer than the rest
one island looms; inexplicable
in the rower's veins, the tide's behest:

Come, come close.   The undiscovered
continent awaits its guest.
This bluff's benignity has suffered

no losses man of man demands.
These firs upon their rocks kelp-covered,
archaic in their formal stance,

hold conifer-coolness in their shade.
Is it their balm on the blue atoll
that draws him on, makes his brows brood

as the rowboat's prow enters the shoals?
Contemplation of that land's
improbable perfection as he poles

the dory on makes him acknowledge
that all that artifice and hands
pride-filled with art's command can manage

of hewing life's rude shapes to grace
the fairness of this sea-spawned image
belittles to its clumsy place.

The seafloor rises.   Now the ledge
that sloped so roundly heretofore
shears above him: splintered ridge

of granite: kelp, browned by the air,
acrawl with snails.   The shattered face
of seacrag echoes toward his ear

dull rattle of muffled knucklebones.
He pries low weeds apart, and peers
in dank crevasses.   Dripping stones:

a skeletal clatter on the floor
writhes with instinct's eruption.
Had not the autumnal moon outpoured

where the lone gull in the low haze lingers
the cold deeps from these shoaled reavings,
none knew those stalkeyed death's avengers.

The rower strains at the rowlocks, heaving
his wake before his face.   The shudder
of waves grips plank and kelson.   Leaving

the script his oars trace on the ocean,
his mind climbs long-accustomed rungs,
from fair forms to fair notions

and thence as Socratic wisdom tongues. . .
Long, long after the dory's keel
grates on the beach and the seadeep gongs

fade in the haze, his mind's swift quills
beat up the bay.   Yet in his veins
crabwise the chilling water crawls.

Exploration

I am who the trail took,
nose of whom I followed,
woodwit I confided in
through thorned-and-briared hallows;
favoring my right side for
clouds the sun had hemmed in.
Behind the North I sought daystar,
bore down highroads hidden
to undiscerning gaze.
My right, my right I turned to
on trails strangely unblazoned
where fistfive forkings burgeoned,
I took my right.   Was destined
among deerdroppings on the ridge
or chipmunk stones astrain
or hoofmucks in the swampcabbage
to err?   Landmarking birch
selfmultiplied in malice till
woods reared a whitebarred cage
around my spinning eye.   The spool
of memory had run out my yarn
and lost the last hank.   Found
I the maze I wander in
where my right, trusted hand,
leads round and round a certain copse,
a sudden mound of stone,
an anthill humming in the rocks

an expectant tune?
Lacklearning now my knowledge is
of how to coax recalcitrant
ignition from cold engines,
or mate a fugue in either hand
on spinet or converse
in any tongue but stonecrop signs.
Clouds hump like battling bulls.   The firs
lash me with angry tines,
shred my clothes.   A windwhipped will
uncompassed, lacking fur or fang,
strange to these parts, yet whom the anthill
anticipating, sang.

The Hermit of Cape Rosier

The hermit of Cape Rosier has three houses:
One's atop the cragged bluff that leaps
splashing spruce out of the water, hackled pines
sawing a jagged hole in heaven.   There
the hermit's house is: no door, windows like wounds,
a ribcage in a hat whose brim is eaves.
You have to know the path up there to find it;
even if you know the old back trail
you have to know the cut-off to the hermit's,
and when you get there, through the thorned blackberries
with the arched gulls shrill in the steep wind
you see   Keep Out   No Trespassing   assigned
on trees and staves.   Perhaps you are not welcome.
'Hello! Hello!' The winds snatch 'Lo!' and dash it
cragward, crumpled, down.   A seahawk's nest
in winter, filled with lichen and picked fishbones
would be as hospitable as is this homestead.
Why would anyone not born to feathers
seek such isolation in the sun?
All that the senses touch up here is cleanly,
scoured by solitude in the harsh height.
Yet grant a hermit reasonable cause
to abjure our fendered comforts, still one might
search his self for the natural parts of man
in scenes more clement.   Not the bleak of air
but ripeness of the earth, in summertime:
sometimes, beneath the blackberries, he searches there.

The second house the hermit lives in
some people wouldn't call a house, unless
sleeping in a cave's compatible
with the human lot.   No one at Harborside
knows what got into Jethro
crouching like a woodchuck in his tunnel
while a scourge of moles rips furrows his father turned.
He's got good lands back there he never touches
except a potato plot and a row of beans;
nobody knows why Jethro won't be seen
at Meeting, store, or trade; nobody knows
just how he lives there, holed up like a marmot
while ruins fall, and hay rises, and teams
move from field to field in hot July.
In woods, in the dead of summer, there's the smell
of green gone sour, of flesh the owl has killed;
delicate leafmould works its webbed decay,
a footstep stirs the leaves, and simmering death
bursts from earth behind a canopy
of green hands, giddy in the wind, that grasp the sun.
The cool of cave-mouth in the hill is dank,
the spindling spider hangs numb from his wheel,
the hemlock-guarded air is cold and still.

The other house the hermit lives in
was once a boathouse, but he has no boat.
You pass clam baskets, broken, pyramided,
and mattocks worn down at the shiny tines,
split oars, stacked driftwood, a pile or two of shells.
Peering through the fogstained saltpocked window
imagine Jethro fingering his trove:
great conches curling empty till his ear brings

15

titanic surfs to tunnels the silent snail
polished in solitude; bright rocks whose stain
of emerald or quartz shaft of shine the starfish
hugged beneath the tide.

Death seems nearer Jethro than it may be,
though in the village they say he's hale and sound.
Life seems precarious on his hillside,
battering windy breakers, by rot deepgnawed,
uncivil, ashake with joy and awe and wonder
at cragged Borealis
and the empty shell left on the shore.

The Beech Tree

The beech tree bristled with hairbone branches,
Twigs between us and the rheumy sky
That wept all winter
And the bare bark ran with rain.
That tree was older than the hoary weather.
By April, though, the leaf-sheaths split and scattered
Showered pods upon the springy ground.
Each day new plenitudes of leaves unpleated
As greening fingers spread their greener fans.
Silent in the summer heat the nuts grew;
We were not aware of them
As the beech tree fended off the August stifle
Under tiered canopies of shade.
The end of summer came by proclamation:
What a tattoo on that tented green!
The nuts have burst their horny husks
And the husks come drumming down!
Now swollen beechnuts are themselves burst—
Cloves and quarters flung by their own swelling
Rat-tat-tatting on each plat of leaves,
Littering the grasses
In unexampled fecundity.
Now comes the onrush from the forest
Soaring lightfoot-leapt acrostics bough to bough
By the hundreds, it would seem, they come to chatter,
Munch and gorge, then, silent, stagger
Logy in repleteness back

To branchy hollows the swooping owl can't find.
At evening, chipmunks dart from deep stone sockets
Busily ferrying beechnuts, cheek by cheekful
Toward crannies winterproof and well-remembered.
Next day the children played at squirrel and chipmunk,
Scooped up beechnuts by the score in baskets,
Scattered and forgot them.

                    Though the leaves
Droop a little in the crisper dawning
And the beech seems skeletal beneath bedecking
And braciness against the icy oncome
Stiffens the stirring of the branches,
The tree, strong-rooted in the changeful weather,
Stands secure against denuding whirlwinds
And the dim glower
Of the rheumy winter sun.

Cowhead

[Transcribed by R. M. Dorson, *Negro Folktales in Michigan*:
Mrs. Smith: I seed that woman with a cowhead on, sure.
Mrs. Richardson. A mighty bad head to carry to Jesus, in my
estimation.]

I dared this.   But love's a power
Makes one risk mockery, lose fear of shame
Or sheer incomprehension. . . One forgets
The unleavened burden of the flesh
Caged in five wits, and the five chimaeras
Those senses take for tangibles.   I came,
I stood before you,—you still garbed in flesh
Loomed within my once-quick womb,—and you,
Your eyes bright beetles in two spoons of ice,
Your hair aspine like daddylonglegs' legs,
Didn't stay to hear me.
You, among that herd in Michigan
Where seed and stalk and flower stretch toward the sun
In sorrowful gestures marking time's demesne,
Could only feel, beneath your breasts, fear's thrill
Like the wind-rung tingle of an icicle,
And never sensed that love that brought me here.
I came,
I tried to tell you—spoke to the heedless cows—
Daughter,
Couldn't you feel the moonshorn in your temples
Throbbing, and the rising in your breasts,
The fecund blood weft in your swelling womb?

19

—I would have told you what his name is,
What his fate.   But let the cornfields reach
Toward heaven.   In ruts beneath their tasseled roof
Of green hair, rumpled by the starry wind,
Predestined seed falls in the waiting warmth.
You will not hear me bless the sprouting issue
Nor know my tongue among the rustling voices;
To one another we cannot speak now,
But in the life that leaps forth fierce to suckle,
Exult and sow seed gaily before its fall
Be power of our communion and our grace.

In Cytherea

She looses, then shakes free her hair.
  Wrists, slim as seabirds' throats,
Waft across the plangent air
  Certain amicable notes.

Her fingers, rippling on the lute
  Like minnows, plunge among the strings;
Her shoulders' curve, the curve of fruit,
  Distracts his mind from what she sings.

He peers through slitted branches bent
  In windows for the shaded spy;
The sun, possessive, insolent,
  Covers her with naked eye.

Coral and alabaster breasts,
  Twin moons, refine that arrant gaze.
O, there his own soul manifests
  Its self as tangible: What praise

Of tongue, of hand what gift or touch
  Could serve as seal of sacrament
To this epiphany, nor smutch
  With smart of earth what's heaven-sent?

Within their hutch of skin, five wits
  Sniff her measure, pace, and twitch.
Who would deny them benefits
  That pleasure soul? They'll have their flitch—

Let soul's ambrosial trencher sate
    Co-tenants in that bower of bone;
Were not all justice insensate
    Should soul, they fasting, feast alone?

The intellect, third triumvir,
    From his cloistral tower comes down,
Adjudicates their sharing her
    To each according to his own.

Joint force confers, resolves, deploys,
    Encircling her from base in bush.
Her song sweetens the wind. . . A noise!
    She starts; the air hums with her hush.

A swoop of knuckles binds lithe wrists,
    His harsh beard briars her breath-stopt throat,
His dizzied senses sweat, she twists,
    They famish, lunge, with glee they gloat

And root for nectar—she rends free,
    Half leaps, half slithers down pell-mell,
Plunges, spuming, in the sea.
    Her long hair streams on the combers' swell.

He lollops across the beaten sands:
    Waves that wreathe impassive rocks
Curl and uncurl in his hands.
    Cold undertows swirl round his hocks.

Safari

You need an empty burlap
bag;   rubber boots;
a forked longhandled stick.
You need nerves like roots

of the willow half underwater
that stiffen the trunk they grip
though that trunk hold boughs aquiver
at the quietest breath.

You kneel on the willow's knees
probing the fern-rimmed ditch
till an arrow furrows the water,
till quiet is cleft by hiss

and quick and true the sinew
tightens in your arm, in your throat
and true and quick the long stick
lunges: a thunderbolt

pinions the diamond head
where the forking tongue is set
immobilizing nothing
else of that undulant jet—

23

I see those brave safaris
and my triumphal returns,
the writhing bag that dangles
from the forked stick's horns,

that dangles over the rosebuds
staked to the trellis I passed,
home through the tended garden
my prize held fast

—'To do *what* with those creatures?
You'll drown them in the drain at once!'—and dream
of a boy, rigid, goggling
down the manhole's gloom

at serpents hugely striding
in the diamonded darkness agleam
and thrashing the still black waters
till they foam and rise like cream.

In the Days of Rin-Tin-Tin

In the days of Rin-Tin-Tin
There was no such thing as sin,
No boymade mischief worth God's wrath
And the good dog dogged the badman's path.

In the nights, the deliquescent horn of Bix
Gave presentiments of the pleasures of sex;
In the Ostrich Walk we walked by twos—
Ja-da, jing-jing, what could we lose?

The Elders mastered The Market, Mah-jongg,
Readily admitted the Victorians wrong,
While Caligari hobbled with his stick and his ghoul
And overtook the Little Fellow on his way to school.

Pot aux Foux

Gérard de Nerval's ribbon led
A large live lobster. Men, like geese
At their communion hissed, or fled,
Made hue, and cried, 'Breach of the peace!'

Enjoined by irate hierarch
He pled *non vult contendere*
'Because,' he said, 'it does not bark
And knows the secrets of the sea.'

Gérard they packed to Dr. Blanche
(Cold-water cures in a year, or less);
The lobster, after that dimanche
When Gendarme's wife served bouillabaisse,

Lost interest in philosophy.
Now Nerval's hung himself, who'll heed
The lucubrations of the sea?
The tides, in bowls, resound, recede.

A Black-Letter Broadside

You convivially swarm
As though to unguent all occasions;
I burn my own heart's bones to warm
The blood that shrinks from soul's abrasions.

My silence is annunciation,
My stillness is the dance of stone,
My gaiety leaps from the blackness
Where I wrest the word alone.

You, in tumultuous nets of voices
Borne by that unrelenting throng,
Cannot escape what blaze rejoices
Me, nor disavow my song.

The Augury

The day my mother came to term
The April air was pure,
Tall dark towers fenced her white bed,
Skylights were barred and dour.

The night my mother got her lamb
There was no moon at all
But a rammed hot rending of her loins
And a babe's red caterwaul

Who fell from darkness into light,
From warmth to time and cold
Bawling for breasts, insatiate,
Already wrinkled-old.

The midwife fingered the still warm caul
In her wishbone-knuckled hands.
In disused mumbles she unspelled
What life such birth portends.

'He shall dance to the serpent's song
As he seeks the dove's dark bower,
And assay to trace Jerusalem
In the crumbs of Babel's tower;

'What gold is his a collar is,
On kennel straw-lain the chain;
What hunger's his a banquet is,
Served from his Father's throne.'

My father raged that a witless crone
Should rant old folly for alms
And turned her out ere she was done;
Scant silver crossed her palm.

What hungers I've since had to taste
Had all the taste of woe,
What wealth into my hands has passed
Buys joys that still seem true,

But still the bird that builds above
The city of my sleep
Broods on a nest of straws.   I move
Half-waking, through a rubbled keep.

Flushing Meadows, 1939

Lightning! Lightning! Lightning! Without thunder!
A zaggedy white trombone of lightshot, crackling
Between metallic globules, egglike, hugely
Aching in the corners of our eyes,—
The afterburn of electrocuted air
Sizzled into our ears and nostrils, halfblinded
Us.   We reeled into the dim sunshine
Groping a little, holding hands, still hearing
The confident vibrant voice of the sound system—
'Harnessed. . . power. . . unnumbered benefits.'. . .'
And this we pondered down the bedecked Concourse
Of Nations.   A gold-robed King of Poland brandished
Crossed swords on horseback pedestaled on high;
The Soviet Citizen bore his sanguine star
Almost as high as that American flag
That snaffled in the smart wind perched atop
The Amusement Park's live parachute drop.
Trapped in antique mores, now the sun
Abandoned the International Pavilions
To miracles of manmade light.   The trees
In their pots were underlit, revealing pasty
Backsides of their embarrassed leaves.   We barked
The shins of our puppylove against the crowds
That swirled around us, swirled like fallen leaves
In the wind's vortex toward the Pool of Fountains:
Mauve and yellowing geysers surged and fell
As national anthems tolled, amity-wise,

From the State of Florida's Spanish Carillon.
What portent, in that luminous night to share
Undyingly, discovery of each other!
Helen, Helen, thy beauty is to me
Like those immutable emblems, huge and pure,—
One glimmering globe the world's will unifying
Beside spired hope that ravels the deep skies,
Our time's unnumbered benefits descrying
In their own light's shimmer, though the new dawn comes
With lightning, lightening in a murmur of summer thunder.

Starlight

When the stars on crystal spheres,
Concupiscent with Heaven, moved,
Such anthems in their light appeared
That aeons burgeoned with their love.

When stars from whirligigs of fire
Were cast by force of mighty laws,
They turned indifferent to desire.
Their light was consequence, not cause.

Stars once from rockets rose, to float
In dalliance, in blaze of joy;
How brightly 'Independence!' wrote
Until they died, that dim July.

Now every season sees them launched
As fire like blood smears Heaven, buoyed
On roaring lights that pour, unstaunched,
New asteroids into the void.

Obedient still to law's strict rule,
What do we by their light divine?
In constellations of the will,
Or discipline to love, they shine.

Awoke into a Dream of Singing

Awoke into a dream of singing.
Birds amassed their gloried peals,
Drenching the deadwood with their ringing.
I could not breathe that air, all song.

Those trees, studded with autumn's plumage,
Bore no leaves that made no sound.
The fountain at their knees cascaded
Icicles.   From brazen wound

The statue gushed.   That air, so chill
With reedy-beaked insistent song,
Clotted fountain's-blood to crystal.
I could not breathe that air, all song.

A Rainride

If sky is water then this train
slithering upon
ribbed driftwood mile on rail
is a whale,

his stomach lined with velvet flesh
meat-red, soft to the touch,
glozing on his bellybone.
I, like Jonah

tried to flee to Tarshish too,
chose not to go
railing round boomtown Nineveh
unpopular dogma.

The stations of the third day come.
Shall I burst from
this bloodblack place of self and leave
the ghost I live

and seek obedient breath to speak
Whose will I wreak?
Or will I yet rebel at dying
and die defying

(when death comes) what Word once lured
me toward rebirth?
Then, then, may the leafy gourd
arise from where I yield to earth.

Sources

'Always check your sources.'
—Professor ———

Before I check my sources
I first must seek them out—
By the mind's prismatic light
That breaks the primal white
To spectral shades which cast
Its primacy in doubt;
My sources I must seek
By that other single beam,
The intuition's blaze:
Wherever that light plays
All things become, or seem,
The aspects of one theme
In metaphor or praise.
These lights that doubly fall
Dazzling point my courses:
Where both beams cross, my soul
Exults to find my sources.

35

Scholiast / Iconoclast

You are absolutely for the relative.
He is resolutely for the absolute.

Your world conforms to what the mind expects,
His world soul's singleness of kind reflects.

His thoughts are feelings and his feelings forms,
Perception's root bears fruit into his arms.

Your thoughts assay the ore of truth in fact
And leave fools gold in the earth that they reject.

I am relatively for the absolute.
My mind sees many while my soul seeks one.

From contraries my soul and mind squeeze truth.
Perception slowly feeds on contradiction.

To be a fabler in an age of fact
Demands a stubborn stomach.   Haut intellect

And soul's intransigent passion may yet compose
The resolute poem that threatens all our prose.

A Triumph

Himself a doctor, knowing all
the toll, the toll each breath exacts,
breathing faster now because the pain
defines the suffering and the end:
It were best to die
as quickly as a breath is stopt
but he must breathe a thousand breaths,
each breath a dying—

I who was there remember
not so much my mother's anguish
nor the emptiness that fell like blows upon the air,
nor the bewildered whimpering of the children,
but the agony of triumph in resignation blazing
in my grandfather's eyes:
Having tried to die he found
that he who seven hundred times had coursed
harsh air through tiny frightened lungs
could not by force of will surrender
the mortal breath that raged within his own.

The Blessings

for Macfarlane

MYRTLE:

My gift is luck,
And when you've heard my charm you'll find
Little enough to do to him.
I sing,

> May no mischance befall you,
> No curse nor sickness gall you;
> From wind's cold lash and heart's despair
> These words I breathe into the air
> You breathe defend you:
>
> Now may your newborn spirit
> No grief, no dole inherit;
> May natural grace your graces feed,
> Fruition be your nurture's meed
> And joys attend you.

This boy's won luck and bounty. You can't harm him.

MORTA:

Very pretty. But here's a little song
To charm him:

> Sleep, little mannikin,
> Wrapt in your little skin.
> That sweeting soul that roundly snores
> Through that infant nose of yours
> Will someday wake, or dream, to know

Its quickened image, nude Ego
Wants all the world's glad rags for clothes;
Ambition's buttons fasten those
That choke contentment tight around
Your heart—the mortal cummerbund.
Nor wisdom staunch its inward itch
Which moral sense will, wretched, scratch.
These blessings come with your first teething.
Such joys you find are my bequeathing.

MOIRA:

Concede the pain. I, like you, concede
The pain of growing and the jagging ache
Denial gnaws upon his ragabone heart.
And yet I say this boy,
Knowing all that, will soon be blessed with joy,
For I shall bless him:

May your dumb five wits feel,
Your five wise senses know,
All life, all death reveal
One Word. Who calls this true?
The Parsee in the Fire,
The Hunted in the Grove—
Their vision, their desire
Its verity avow.
The cradled infant dreams
In the unity of their sight,
In the sleeping lover teems
Their intellectual delight,
The Dying Hero's might
From loss their Word redeems:
Read the hieroglyph aright,
All tongues together choir
The syllables of Love.

MORTA:

That's noble, sister, but I'll spell you down.
That mother's-milk and love-making routine
With the ever-fashionable sacrifice
To make the last act holy is a dream.
Aren't you the sentimentalist! This boy is
Fated to be handled by realities.
I've got a tune for his condition. Here's
A lullaby—

Lully, lullay,
You'll sleep, and sleep,
And wake, and weep.
You'll wake, to seek
Simplicity,
The lodestar of
Felicity,
But dreams will prove
Truth self-divides.
Lullay, lully,
Multiplicity
Taunts, derides
The simple soul
That seeks the Whole.
You'll sleep and sleep
Nor mind may rest
That I have blessed.

Bye, bye, bye,
Now that you lie
Under a Heaven
That's soiled and riven
By too many moons,
All bolts that threaten
Impiety

Are boons self-given
To men who've beaten
Ploughshares and hearts
In the natural way.
What reason fashions
By generous law
Your anarch passions
Will rend and gnaw
While affections' arts
In cold thought decay.
Lully, lullay.

FATHER:

To these their blessings I will add my blessing·

     I'll bless you, Son, with all the might our mortal
Franchise makes us heir to. The immortal

Possibility, the healing Whole,
Your Spirits offered to your hungering soul;

Your Norn, the incubus: Three most ripe fruits,
Heedless of thorns that stem all Absolutes.

     The fruit I proffer's tougher: the protean splendor
Of mortal possibility, bestowing,

In the sacramental urgency of growing,
Hallows on its constant apprehender.

     Accessible to pain's finality,
To unclad selfhood's meteoric claw,

Imagination's prodigality
An orbit past finality can draw

To trace the trials of mortal joy. The power
That transubstantiates your spikenard days

Of hived disorder that in Nature swarms
Be all my benison: All your assays

In passion find, and shape in thought, the forms
Of love and the anatomies of praise.

My voice woke up the baby and he cried.
His mother gave him suck. He slept content,
A miniscule of manhood. The fontanelle
Pulsed under his fuzz, moving a little.

TALIESIN

'The text records the fiction of which
Taliesin is the hero. . . . No perfect
copy of the Mabinogi of Taliesin being
accessible, it has been necessary to print
it in the present series from two frag-
ments. . . . The MS. is of quarto size.'

—LADY GUEST, Notes to *Taliesin* (1848).

Taliesin

1. Wry Bread

'None shall enter save
king or son of a king
or craftsman bearing his craft.'

One, a cobbler carrying his cobbleskills,
Another, princed by heraldic ghosts,
And the haut bard Taliesin
Broke bread of many hosts.

When place and power are generalized
And magnificence is unmeet
And craftsmanship's anomaly
As gold for goosegirl's feet,

As goosegirl is, as poet,
Taliesin, who did know
All Nature's secrets may incant
Hungry these shall go.

ii. Taliesin Sings

O, Everyman is King.   No
Nobleness.   All flats are courts.
The College of Druids is out of work
Here.   The sun's out of sorts

With the seasons.   Men walk about
Bearing the same blood under their skins
That once was schooled in bardic
And political disciplines;

To this people gorged on rhetoric's tongue
Whose governance is popularity's
Encomium, I in my age too long
Cast these prophecies.

iii. Divinations of Taliesin

*

'Tis hard for the dwarf geometer to drink
Despite mindmastery of Euclid's doubts
And th'infallible Pythagorean rule
A toast at the banquet-table of the gods

Without a ladder propped against the stool.

＊　　　＊

Popularity's encomium:
'The hiatus of singular eminence'
Repels; th'Elect rise on the piety
Due those images which reflect
The multitude's homogeneity.

＊

＊　　　＊

Eagles bleated at his birth,
Planets shone, voids sighed.
O at his advent heaven and earth
Ached for Destiny.   He came, he cried,

He grew that figure magisterial
'Mong clerks and salespersons; learned much;
Spurred by ambitions empyreal,
Prepared.   He got the common touch,

Talisman of power and place.
For interest, he is just in governance;
Distinction's face now wears his face,
In ward after ward after ward, redundance.

Two Hundred Girls in tights & halters
Cowboyboots cutaway at the calves
White plumes jiggling from their helmets
Make Main Street swagger in a dream

Four Hundred Bluebreasts bound in bronze
Bodies follow a twirling stave of steel
In unison 'Beethoven's Moonlight Sonata' playing
Each on her shining glockenspiel.

Love, under the circumstances,
Is tooled to new designs;
Not passional intensity; consensus
Settles for less, and finds
Cowgirls' unanimity enhances
Their chances.

Not potion in the coffeecup
Nor harrowing, for love, the grave
To restore all losses; for unlost
To doom's tall grandeur, those who crave
The cheerled joys of playing host
To such advances.

The artist of 'The Beautiful'

Will dream of kumquats, but he'll dine
On pickles, kippers, and saltines,
Feeling that that austerity
Is truer to his own integrity
As well as what is best within his means.

Kumquats, receding in his dreams,
Grow flat, and round, despised as gold.
He'll come to glory in his station:
A voluptuary of abnegation
Who broils in sensual heat when his feet are cold.

All Nature's secrets
Became my ken
Not through cunning.
Caridwen
Set hands of Gwion's
To stir her soup
Of inspiration, Science,

And Grace.   One drop
Of each splashed my thumb,
Pain made me taste;
Gwion's become
Taliesin,
'Radiant brow,'
Who till now
Was unlearned and chaste.

Once out of nature
Man shall never take
Solace or self-measure
Nor shall he slake
His prodigious thirst
To swill her broth,
Chew grounds for treasure.
Some gulped Inspiration,
Some Science, some both,
Famished for power or honour.
I who nothing sought
By thumb's unlucky thrust
Drew a richer draught.
Of all I was given,
I would I were shriven.

When sound leaps slow and
Lightning dimly
Babe and crone and maiden cower
Beneath smashed chimney.

Do I speak truth, then let consume
These starlings of my song with flame,
And naught hatch from the shell's ash
In the cindered skull's mausoleum.

*

Someday, perhaps, the race will go
Both to the swift and to the slow.
Then we shall find that great belief
Round Stonehenge chaunted long ago,
Before the mind and heart to grief
Did fall because man willed it so.

Caridwen, be my Muse; my theme,
How man, born out of beasts' embrace
To stride toward death, wills to redeem
His days by love and mind and grace,
And finds, where buds and maggots teem
In the ceaseless sun, his natural place.

Gold for the goosegirl—
That's a generous song.
Transgresses accustomed deprivations,
But love's not powerless. A wrong
Descried against appearance?
These waddling fowl detain
One whose most casual motion proves
How ineluctable is beauty's reign;

A wrong against reality:
Her slender shoulder, in repose,
Shames all professions of regality
That call her less. These gold-wrought shoes
Are hers! Who casts such beauty down
Contra naturam I defy his wrong.
Lady, for whose love I'll dare all,
—Out of my way, geese—I bring thee song.

There is but one for whom I make this song.
For her the cockerel sun in honey steeps
His sheaves of light that rise like summer grain—
He'd sow the world with light, to gaze on her!
O when she turns, the whole sky turns with her.
She seethes the malty marrow of my blood;
I, just to watch her, feel my rooted soul
Whirl, a green tall dizzying Maypole.

O what a gallantry of grace attends
The slightest dancing of her wrists and knees—
I had not thought that Nature or my kind
Could bear within our frangible human form
Such annunciation.   Where she comes
Combs of honey burst on my five wits;
I can relive it all, all hallowing:
Merely to think upon her is to sing.

O when I think then how she closer came—
The air I breathed glowed in her aureole
—Then all her motion was a scarf of wind;
I leaned her toward me, and her long arms clung
And body moved with body, mind with mind
Annealed while thought and motion surged in flame
That feeds upon, yet feeds, root, trunk, leafed poll:
It was that incandescence forged my song.

In the sun's resplendency
Magnificence is generalized.
From the sky's cerulean intensity
The dazzled gaze
Drops down, to rise:
    Heroic images reflect
Possibility's largesse
Where every fact and artifact
Exalt in man's imagining.
Here stones show nobleness
And every man is king.

The court recedes
In measured pace,
Ascendant flags define the true
Perspectives of the royal place.
      The stance of a man

                        may seem
Belittled where in grandeur tall
Equestrian statues raise
The prance of granite plumes aspiring
      Half in heaven,
Rear hooves yet rooted in the earth;

      The man who stands
Below them has the earth for pedestal,
Half in heaven

                  his eyes leap toward the sun
Guyed upward, as those hooves' compulsion
To leap is upward,
                  as the stone,
Hammer-humbled to submission
By craftsmanship and intellect,
Baffles the natural fact
And leaps,

                  leaps upward like his eyes
Half in heaven, toward the sun.

          *

     *   *

  *   *   *

Who brings idealization
          to this rock?
The hand that held the hammer?
          the calculable blows it struck,
Or the life whose realization
          is here intensified?

          What image or imagining
This stone reflects
          of man, who brings into his art
Magnificence, or resplendency
          of art brings to his acts.

     *   *

  *   *   *

     *   *

You dispraise my vision in that moral sense
Should not a horseback warlike man select
For an apothegm in stone?
You, then, would instead erect
A mirror to the multitudes of love
And liberally reject
All reflection that man's violence
Has to do with what perfection
He is capable of?

Were I who have endured my age too long to wait
For Adam's second coming without lust
I might envision the wholly perfect state.
For love I praise with all my passion
But do distrust
Moral rhetoric gorged on abnegation.
The knowledge burnt into my brain is that
Perfect justice is unjust;
I deal in nature, and accommodate
All that seethes in blood and must.
Perfection I proclaim as what
Passion and discipline create
When necessity and joy adjust
What's possible to the moral sense.
I'll stand requital for what wrongs
My horseman does to excellence
When states are made as well as songs.

      ✦   ✦   ✦

    ✦   ✦   ✦   ✦

           ✦

This wind in the wool
Tickles shepherd and sheep;
Its itch roils their sleep.
Whoever scratches is mortal.

Do I speak truth
Then let this breath deny
As much of death
As any man can. I
My burnt tongue's gift bequeath
To you in whom my speech
Or song moves most:
Act, enact the myth
Of man the maker: Reach
In every syllable
Of your life, in each
Motion of your soul
As though these dreams my ghost
Long since made were real;
Such magnificence you touch
Shall your self become.
At the portal of your feast
I sing, though dust be dumb:
Praise the immortal host,
Mortal encomium

A LITTLE GESTE

A Little Geste

1. Near Nottingham

The wry contrarieties
Of pomegranate and hock
Suggest, to the friar at ease
After mendicant's luck,
That the stranger, who'd pluck
Viands such as these
From a doeskin sack
As he knelt near the trees
And shared rare courtesies
And nought did the bag lack
While he spelled liturgies
As though by a Book—
Could tell tales that unlock
Arcane verities;
Their mad might would mock
His poor hagiolatries.
The fruit burns. He tries
To quench from wine-crock;
Fumed ferments arise;
His brainbands unlock.
Wits seethe through his shock
Of iced hair: His brows freeze
In the agate-eyed look

That beholds black epiphanies
And the flat world never sees
As before.   Dazed awake,
Famished for mysteries
That green tongue could speak
—What road did he take?
His rood he doth seize
And forth leaps Friar Tuck—
Which way? Through those trees?

II. Chant

We hunted the wren for Robin the Bobbin,
We hunted the wren for him alone,
We hunted the wren for the Hooded Robin,
We hunted the wren for every one.

Whose arrow was it burst
The wren's thighbone and heart?
It was the Robin's dart,
The blood is on his breast,

The blood is on the brown dry grass,
It glistens in the sun,
Its sprouts leap from the thawing earth,

We hunted the wren for every one.

iii. Aubade

White Pater Noster,
God by my Foster.
> Foster me as thy oak tree
> Cloaked in mistletoe
> Greenless winter doth despite
> (Though greenleaves shrivel in the sky)
> With golden seed and bough.
> Like oak, like mistletoe and yew
> Foster me.

As I am made of flesh and blood
God send me my right food.
> Send me food as thou send good
> Goldseed to Robin and Wren.
> Keep the firmament all full
> With our sacramental meal:
> Springpods burst and larvae split,
> On the greenboughs winged gods flit,
> And so feed me.

In the crimson corner of the year
God keep all ills far from here.

  Keep ills far from those who love
  Oak, robin, wren.
  To them to whom their ways are known
  As the blood in the bone's home
  Foreknows that inward hour when death
  In immolation seeks rebirth,
  Keep ills away.

Thrice I strike with holy crook,
For Wren, for Robin, and for Lok.

  For goldcrowned wren, the old year's lord
  In misrule whirls about.
  The heavens whirl, until his thigh
  Pierced by my arrow be,
  Till hung, till eaten he. For Luck
  I strike. For me.

IV. The Lay of Marian

Some were knotting their nets,
    some seined the replenishing sea,
the weir closed off the harbor,
    white water wild in the web.
No ship nor shape could enter
    and the whole town teemed to the quays
and prayed as the year's provender
    the fishermen shored from the shoals.
I, at the tidehead's elbow
    whitelegged on my sacks of flour,
driving my mare to market
    saw the struggle outshore
and the calm reflect the near rushes.
    Not a ripple nor plash shook the scene,
and then—by the Virgin I swear,
    at the head of the tide by the water
I saw her, standing there.

Once, bringing my flour to the castle,
    I saw, through an open door
a court of fair ladies adancing,
    dukes' damsels and vavasours'.
Many a month I remembered
    the white small arms of one,
remembered so hard that I doubted
    flesh formed so fair as my dream,
till at the tide's head I saw her.
    Since then, if my white-armed fair

should say, 'Although I am a countess
    Come to me, Much,' I'd not come.
For *she* stood in the sunlight, unmoving
    save her steeplehat's burgeoning veil
green as the wings of a mayfly,
    in her green gown gauded with pearl.
My knees pushed the ground, my heart knelled
    the dooms of my sins in my ears—
'O Queen of Heaven, why comest'ou
    before this poor miller's son—'
'Fear me not, Much,' she said in a singing
    tongue of delight, and her hand
tousled my hair.   'Rise and take me
    to Him.'   We came here.

WILL SCARLET:

As I stalked
the king's red deer
I had less luck
than I had ale,
and my tongue's thirst
had less to drink
than my holey pocket
held farthings.
When axle squeals
pierced my ears
I knew I'd lost
my buck, and swore.
I heard stems crush,
heard boughs snap short,
thought of my buck
in some far thicket,
yet looked straight about
and knew before I saw—
this twelve-tined stag
paused right before
my arrow sprang,
drew taut and twanged,
straight to the heart.
Like a wall, like a tower
he tottered and fell.
Then came the cart.

This fellow Much
on his pasty legs
walked before
that ragabone horse
and his load of flour,
and there, on his seat
supple as a doe
but proud and veiled
like a tall green willow
she sat
in silence.

I fear no woman,
at the Nottingham fair
I've squeezed the girls,
the round backsides
and bosom's plums
of many a Jill
fit snug in my hand.
I can draw the bow
with the longest span
in the country round,
I fear no woman.

But why did I find
my knees touch the ground,
my head inclined,
my quick tongue
sausage-thick in the mouth?
And when she laughed,
'Rise, Will.   Come.'
I felt no shame
but like a tame
jackdaw threw
my game upon the cart—
and came.
Why does the blood
from my head to groin
pound and surge
and promise joy?

Lady,

Longtime ere now before my second birth
I fabled so to the credulous multitude
That mired to the crotch in mud, they held the earth
To be but platform, and their acts, prelude
—As shepherds on the church porch make cold mirth—
Awaiting, in the snow, beatitude.

When roistering plowman, wanton, all that brood
Of wenching dicer, goodwife, ribald dame,
Like flies round carrion congregated loud
Where mountebanks and merchants trapped fair game,
I'd mount some tinker's waggon, raise my rood
And cry, Harrow! at all their traffic's shame,

And shame them for their trivial passions, blame
Those lusts that baste the brain beneath the snood
For their unworthiness.   O man, to maim
Thy half-angelic soul, to limp in lewd
Round dances when by birthright thou should claim
The passional glory of Christ's Holihood—

My voice would drop then, like His dropping blood,
Then rise and pour upon them, as the firth
Roars inward with the tide's returning flood,
Bearing the ancient promise of rebirth
Would they but follow where He bore their rood . . .
But now my sermons all are nothing worth.

Golgotha towered above them, yet the earth
Must all that's mortal mercilessly reclaim;
God's counsel of perfection I pealed forth
Yet all who heard I saw revert to shame
And lunge toward tavern or defile the hearth
And priests and monks, like tinkers, did the same.

Heartsick at man's mortality, I came
Trudging through a darkly verdant wood;
Nor inner fire of my belief, nor flame
Of holy rhetoric had ever showed
Another's soul, nor mine—and mine the blame—
The lasting way to the slain Son's Holihood.

Disconsolate I trudged that darkening wood
When from the ground I sensed there looming forth
A presence, huge, horn-helmed, green-clad.   I stood
Like stone; he took a doe's sack from his girth
And smiling, gave me wine, and fruit for food
Somehow unearthly, yet redolent of earth—

He vanished.   Annunciation pierced me.   Forth
I plunged to seek Him, serve Him, by what Name
His Godhead goes to chant the world's rebirth.
Stumbling through brambles, toward this cart I came
Lured past bracken by sound of human mirth,
And found you, Lady, and the meal, the game,

And found the staff I walk with rise in flame
And leaves burst from this long-dead oaken wood
And I knelt, knowing now His Name, your Name
O Maid and Mother, and laid my flowering rod
Beside you, next the stag, the sack, and came
With you, and Will, and Much, to Robin Hood.

v. The Coming of Robin Hood

Given: that glebe   and gorse and groundsel
be seared by scorch   of the merciless sun;
that hillock and ridge   rust, through rainwater
is none: that North,   nimbus the wood needs
grind like a grate   high over the ground;
that ash of dead fires   from dark heavens falling
make scape of land sea,   while snowtide reveals
nor furrows deepfilled   nor furze nor flower.
Here in the sameness   of space is horizon
in an age of dying.   But deep in the heavens
sinuous surges   of sun prick the crystal
and sink to earth's center;   sap stirs
in blood as in root   with burgeon and budding.
The ground heaves, and green   is the girth of the meadow
                    for now
            the sun-faced groundsel beams;
            in seedfields, row on row
            of greenlanced barley teems.
            Gorse drinks the melting snow.

Besought: from unstinting   sun, from the seasons,
phoenixes four   ever fecund returning,
from kestrel and crab,   from kine, from tall corn,
from all that is born   to bequeath its beginning,
to share in the source   of that ceaseless strength,
to feel the energy   under the flesh
rise in the rhythm   of the world's return.
But witness are we   that wane of winter
precedes the singing   of cuckoo in sedge,
that greenbriar bursts   through a compost grave.

All that's alive   is enfeoffed to the dead.
Death quitclaims none   yet conquers never;
the egg's in the ash,   ever inviolate.
O Sovereign Source   Whom we beseech
of Life-in-Death   and Death-in-Life,
deliver us, unworthy,   to worship thy works,
permit us to praise   with our tongues thy powers,
to see thy divinity   dwell in our shape
                              as a man
              whose holy human breath
              and speech is ours, who can
              endure His life and death
              in septuagennial span.

Moves among us   a miracle maker,
came on a winey   wind to call
into this forest   His faithful forth.
At crest of moon   the coven convenes:
black sky's scaled   by bonefire: sun
recalled to burn   bleak night to day.
With besom He beats   the deathdark back,
beckons with brand   His band to the light.
Now skirl of pipes   and skittle of bones
hymns our homage   in halidom wild.
In laughter and love   life's force we praise,
cleft foot, calved foot   cross round cauldron
and merry the mirth   that mingles with mounting
                          flame
              in prothalamium:
              The God in Man whose name
              we cry at last has come
              His marriage rite to claim.

Round and round   goes ring and round
in the holy stations   of the Sun.
Submagus Tuck   the ember takes,
chanting, 'Fire,   O fecund source
of life returning,   burn, eternal
Sun and soul!'   The circle third
is finished. Flame   the Friar replaces.
Bread he beckons   and breaks. The ram
this morning spitted   is served and spent.
Now Robin waves,   winecasks come:
goodwives, Maid,   their God and men
mingle mortal   joy and make

their meal,
sing 'Robin, Marian, bless
thy supplicants with weal,
Foster our happiness
who do Thy praises peal!'

To skittle and skirl   now wheels and skips
in skimble-skamble   scamper spinning
through murk of must   and moon's-horn dusk
the dance! Toward trance,   toward transformation
they leap and rush,   reel and tremble:
Tuck whispers, hoarse,   'A hare am I!
Take me, earth!'   and down he tumbles.
Leaps to the sky   Long John! Will
seizes Suky and   somersaults!
Much wafts his hands: 'I'm windblown wheat;
I beckon thee, birds,   devour my body!'
Robin spreads wide   wings: 'The sparrow
That last year gobbled   thy grain I slew.
You're free!' Then Marian   falls on fours,
rears, and whinnies,   'The world I'll foal!'
Bonebonds wrought   to wraiths of will
they run, soar,   swim, conjoin
in images bursting   brain and blood,
as thew and thigh   and thought rejoice,
                              and rise
                  bodied forth as fanes
                  wherein each lover lies
                  stag-strong and scarlet stains
                  the whiteness of her thighs.

Tongues pierce inward,   redly touching:
in glade where gladness   gushed in a ground
faggots' crackle   fades, hissing;
alone the woodlouse   reels on the log.
Clouds of stars   crinkle in heaven;
a nightjar burbles   belated rills;
murmuring leaves,   murmuring grasses;
the dark moves in;   a muffled sigh,
a breath in sleep's   instinctual stirring:
—this scene the ember's   eye regards.
Sounds of silence   stroke the forest—
ratchet of claws,   birdwings' rustle,
a wind of waking   wafts the halflight.
Under the briery   bush the bride
slumbers still   beyond all sorrows.
Horned groom, god   or halfgod, softly
sunders from her,   in own self shapen.
What does he see   in the ember staring?
Passes green fingers   through yesternight's flames:
                          from nest
             of ash tall cock thrice crows:
             Sun leaps from East to West.
             All's well.   Each homeward goes
             singing, renewed, and blessed.

VI. A Ballad of Robin Hood and the Prioress

Busk ye, bowne ye, merrymen all
    To Robin's holy tree.
His staghorn helm, his besom tall
    And roe's cloak beareth he.

'O Master,' asketh Little John,
    'What longing agues thy bones?'
'I cannot rest with my merrymen,
    Or dry wombs plague thy sons.

'The mortal breath within me wanes
    And I my covenant keep;
To the nunhouse where the prioress reigns,
    Her leechcraft must I seek.'

'O I mislike her cruel white mouth
    That tastes not of our wine,
Slim throat she masks in monkish cowl—'
    'Ah, farewell, Little John.'

Look, o look, the women weep
    On Robin's either side,
Their tears salt down the dry road's dust,
    His name it is they cry.

Robin has gone within the gate,
  The leech she's brought to him,
First she bleeds the thick red blood,
  Then she bleeds the thin.

Never a drop of Robin's blood
  She lets fall on the ground,
Merryman's horn, the dim green wood
  Whirl round him in a swound.

Never a drop that Robin bleeds
  On Marian's thighs shall fall;
The prioress clicks her eyeballbeads.
  His wounds will never heal.

VII. Tuck, in the Stocks

The faggots are gathering.   Marian's din
Slits my ears.   They've stript her,
Flayed her with hazelwood, raised
Gutters of blood on her thighs.
Her curses tell them
Nothing.   Me they save
For later devisings; wry contrarieties
Boil in my brain.   I see
Things no one has seen—

> Bonefire light is candlelight
> In waxbrained pumpkinskull;
> Wither, wither, Beltane rites
> Beneath Tuck's tattered cowl:
> I who shifted shapes with hare,
> Master with the holy bird
> When nickering Marian played the mare
> Whom all we twelve adored—
> Children reenact our doom
> As goblins, crooked crone
> Falsefaced, mischievously roam
> Under the bleeding moon;
>   What virtue hath the sun?

Little John turns, turns, turns, turns on the rack
Waiting.   Four cropped stallions chomp the branches, waiting
At the great crossroads to the world's far corners.
His limbs each bound to each one's back they
Spur them—his joints spurt—
For the renegade friar such clerks devise
Ingenuities more rare.   My eyes
Burn, burn on the unforgiving scene—

       Virgins grasp their grapey god,
       Rend him from his bones,
       Devour divinity in his blood,
       Carry him in their loins
       Mothering more than merely man;
       Within an oaken glade
       Let godhead for a day be Wren
       In Master Robin's stead.
       The goatgod, his mad Maenads fade,
       The green world turns to stone,
       No sacrifices made,
       Sacred trees hewn down.
          What virtue hath the sun?

In the Iron Maiden Scarlet Will the bowman
Who rolled his merrimaids under the briary bush
Groans in the barbed spikes' embraces.
Robin's goodmen, in fast love, in faith
Let vile deaths seal their secrets in.
O love I bear Him, bolt my jaw—
But first these men of the iron cross
I blast: All anguish chew their seed.

        The greencapped forester, our dear lord,
        To democratic thief
        Through fame's and history's reward
        Shrinks.   None shares our grief.
        But children, chanting Eeny Mo,
        Dimly remember us,
        Although the Eucharistic dough
        And unfermented juice
        Affirm a taste for crackermeal;
        Transubstantiated blood
        Runs thin.   Indifferent seasons wheel
        Till man again will die as god
          And virtue hath the sun.

VIII. A Carol of the Birds

The one that pulled the thorn
God's bloodstain ever since has worn.
The one in wintry ivy
Keeps the New Year's song alive.

From thorns one hangs his kill.
His flowers in feathers bloom, all still.
Another crops the seed
We've sown against our mortal need.

The robin and the wren
Are God Almighty's cock & hen,
The shrike and the sparrow
Are the Devil's bow & arrow.

God send to us such birds
As our charity deserves.
Pray wren's and robin's nests
Enlarge His mercies in our midsts,

While birds of baneful feather
We'll lime and throttle all together
And hang each poisoned sparrow's corse
From thorns the shrike haunts in the gorse.